Positive Care

Look in the mirror
and say 5 positive
things about your
appearance

Positive Thoughts

What have you done for someone else recently that made you feel good?:

Positive Actions

Join a club or group or
attend a class/session

Positive Words

Repeat the following affirmation to yourself 5 times upon waking and before bed:

I will not worry about things I cannot control

Positive Care

Try some guided
meditation or guided
breathing exercises

Positive Actions

Write a to do list for the
day and tick off each item
as you complete it

Positive Thoughts

Who is the most positive person you know? How do they make you feel?:

Positive Care

Give yourself or get a
hand or foot massage

Positive Words

Repeat the following affirmation to yourself 5 times upon waking and before bed:

I will treat myself with the same respect that I give to others

Positive Thoughts

What mantra would be most useful to you? Write it down:

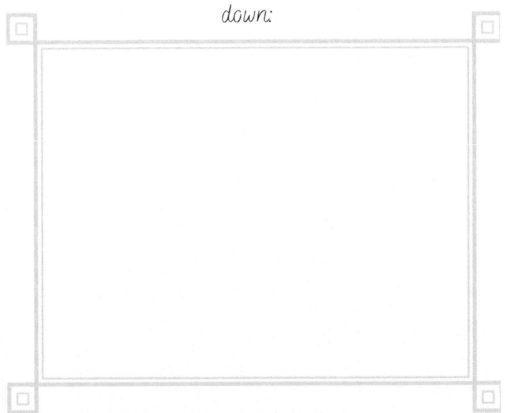

Positive Actions

Celebrate an achievement
or special occasion with
someone

Positive Words

Repeat the following affirmation to yourself 5 times upon waking and before bed:

I will be kind to myself and allow myself to hope

Positive Care

Arrange a visit or
outing with friend or
family member

Positive Thoughts

Write about a time you overcame an obstacle that was difficult:

Positive Words

Repeat the following affirmation to yourself 5 times upon waking and before bed:

I am worthy of my dreams

Positive Actions

Re-organise/clean your
environment such as your
bedroom or where you spend a lot
of time

Positive Care

Try writing your own poetry about positive thinking or watch a TED talk on positive mindsets

Positive Thoughts

What is the nicest thing someone has said about you? How does it make you feel?

Positive Actions

Sort emails or phone apps to help clear and organise one of your spaces

Positive Words

Repeat the following affirmation to yourself 5 times upon waking and before bed:

Good things can and will happen for me

Positive Care

Find a calming or happy scent for your room like a candle or reed diffuser

Positive Thoughts

What would be on your bucket list? Can you start working on any of these?:

Positive Actions

Read a self-help or self-improvement book or e-book

Positive Words

Repeat the following affirmation to yourself 5 times upon waking and before bed:

It not other people's job to like me, it's mine and I love myself a little more each day

Positive Care

Have a zero negativity
day. Strive to
approach everything
in a positive light and
avoid making
criticisms

Positive Thoughts

What have you learned about yourself recently?:

Positive Actions

Plant something or purchase a
plant to nurture

Positive Words

Repeat the following affirmation to yourself 5 times upon waking and before bed:

I will act intuitively and trust in myself

Positive Care

Treat yourself with something you will appreciate e.g. a comfort meal, a beauty treatment or some new clothing

Positive Actions

Invest in a hobby, be it something
to do with DIY, arts & crafts,
horse riding gear etc... support an
interest that you really enjoy

Positive Thoughts

What scares you and why? Is there anything you can do to minimise that?::

Positive Care

Plan and take
yourself out on a date
e.g. dinner, coffee
date, cinema etc..

Positive Words

Repeat the following affirmation to yourself 5 times upon waking and before bed:

I let go of anything that doesn't serve me well

Positive Thoughts

How are you feeling today? Why? If it's negative what can you do to make it better?:

Positive Actions

Make a mood boosting play list

Positive Thoughts

Write 5 ways you can combat your own stress:

Positive Care

Watch something that
makes you laugh
deeply

Positive Actions

Challenge any negative self talk
i.e. if you find yourself thinking or
saying anything negative about
yourself take a moment to correct
the statement into a positive as
you would for a friend

Positive Words

Repeat the following affirmation to yourself 5 times upon waking and before bed:

I deserve happiness, I trust the process

Positive Actions

Try something new, it can be an activity, a place, a type of food. The point is to try something unfamiliar that you may enjoy or are curious about

Positive Thoughts

What things make you smile?:

Positive Actions

Listen to some music from your favourite years, something that incites nostalgia and enjoyment

Positive Care

Remove any negative
social media you are
following and find
some positive
accounts to follow

Positive Words

Repeat the following affirmation to yourself 5 times upon waking and before bed:

I am whole, I am blessed, I know my worth

Positive Thoughts

How would your best friend describe you?:

Positive Thoughts

What are your top 3 priorities in life? Do any of these need more attention?:

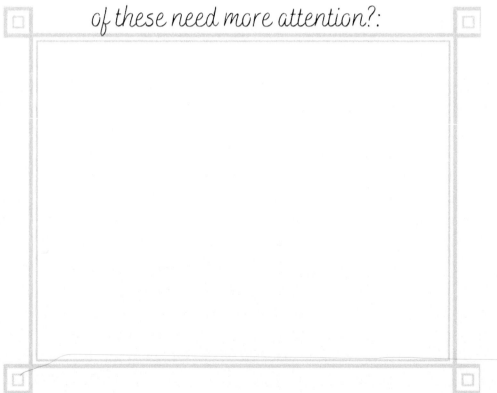

Positive Actions

Learn something new, it can be anything from a simple recipe or skill to learning a new language

Positive Thoughts

What is your best memory?:

COLOURING IN

Take some time to let your mind wander...

Positive Thoughts

What good or healthy habits could you add to your life?:

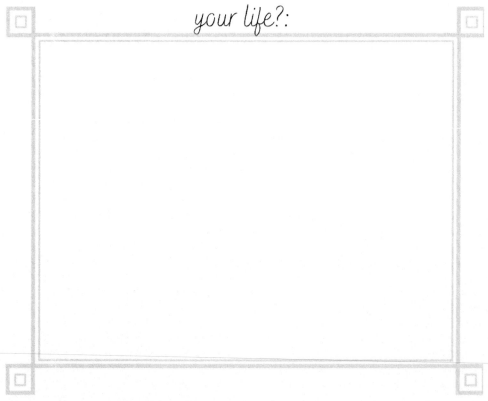

Positive choices

Choose positive statements to replace negative ones:

E.g. I can't do this ➡️ with practice I can get better at this

Positive Thoughts

What bad habits would you like to quit and how would you do that?:

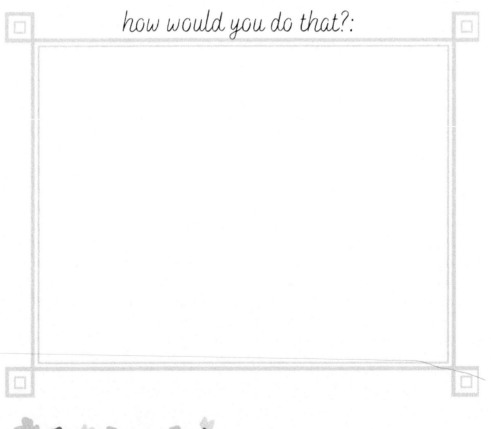

Positive Actions

Have a pamper day however that looks for you e.g. facial, hair mask, nails, body scrubs etc.... the choice is yours as to what you will enjoy the most

Positive Thoughts

What can you forgive yourself for?:

Positive Words

Repeat the following affirmation to yourself 5 times upon waking and before bed:

I have a voice and that voice matters

Positive Actions

Watch the sunrise or sunset and
take time to appreciate it

Positive Words

Repeat the following affirmation to yourself 5 times upon waking and before bed:

I am the author of my own story

Positive Thoughts

How can you make tomorrow better?:

Positive Words

Repeat the following affirmation to yourself 5 times upon waking and before bed:

I challenge myself to grow and every day brings an opportunity

Positive Thoughts

What would your dream life look like?:

Positive Words

Repeat the following affirmation to yourself 5 times upon waking and before bed:

I have the power to create change

Positive Thoughts

Write yourself 3 compliments:

Positive Actions

De-clutter your wardrobe. Make a "keep" pile, a "maybe" pile and a "go" pile. The "go" pile can be offered to charity or friends or sold. Take time with the "maybe" pile and think about enlisting a friend or family member as you try on items and decide whether to keep them or let them go.

Positive Words

Repeat the following affirmation to yourself 5 times upon waking and before bed:

I strive to be the best version of myself, I can do it, I trust in me

Positive Thoughts

What do you love most about your life at the moment?:

Positive Questions

What 3 things would you like to change in your life?

What steps or goals can you take to help achieve this?

Positive Care

Take a switch off day
and choose to do
something you enjoy
for relaxation e.g.
watch a movie, read a
book, listen to a
podcast etc..

Positive Intake

Aim to drink 2 litres/8 cups
of water today or find/make
a nourishing drink like a
smoothie

Positive Actions

Write your "past self" a letter.
Be forgiving of any mistakes,
show praise for achievements
and show compassinnate care
for any difficulties

Positive choices

Select a choice & follow it:

I will get my body moving for 10 mins by trying:

Some yoga

Dancing

Stretching

Bike riding

Jogging

Positive Words

Repeat the following affirmation to yourself 5 times upon waking and before bed:

I am growing through every experience and each day provides a new lesson

Positive Actions

Do something nice for someone e.g. bake them a cake, bring them flowers, write them a thank you note etc...

Positive Intake

Find a new recipe and make
yourself a healthy balanced
meal with plenty of colour
from different
vegetables/fruits

Positive Thoughts

Write down 4 things you are really good at:

Positive Care

Get creative! Try writing, drawing or painting

POSITIVITY WORDSEARCH

I	E	E	P	R	P	A	W	E	D	G	I	I	E
S	U	N	A	E	A	U	T	H	E	N	T	I	C
T	T	I	T	F	L	L	I	K	I	N	D	M	T
R	P	N	I	H	C	B	V	E	T	S	D	P	E
E	H	A	E	F	E	S	A	N	V	I	T	G	C
N	I	E	N	U	S	M	T	I	I	S	F	G	N
G	C	T	T	N	G	T	A	E	L	H	R	S	E
T	H	O	U	G	H	T	F	U	L	E	T	M	D
H	T	C	I	E	I	A	C	N	I	H	R	I	I
A	A	S	S	E	R	T	I	V	E	R	L	L	F
P	V	H	O	N	E	S	T	H	Y	U	T	E	N
P	T	N	V	S	G	N	I	R	A	C	N	T	O
Y	L	K	T	U	Y	H	T	R	O	W	K	L	C
H	E	E	C	B	E	V	I	T	A	E	R	C	C

FUN
THOUGHTFUL
RELIABLE
ASSERTIVE
WORTHY
CONFIDENCE
CARING
SMILE
CREATIVE

AUTHENTIC
STRENGTH
KIND
PATIENT
HAPPY
HONEST

Positive Words

Repeat the following affirmation to yourself 5 times upon waking and before bed:

I can achieve anything I put my mind to

Positive choices

Select a choice & follow it:

I will start a new:

Morning routine ☐

Evening routine ☐

For that routine I will:

_____

_____

_____

_____

_____

COLOURING IN

Take some time.....

Positive Care

Get some more rest by
going to bed earlier or
having a lie in

Positive Words

Repeat the following affirmation to yourself 5 times upon waking and before bed:

I am doing my best and my best is good enough

Positive Thoughts

What things/people make you the most happiest and why?:

Positive Actions

Go out for a coffee on your
own or invite someone along.

Positive Care

Make list of things you
want to do and how you
can work towards them

Positive Words

Repeat the following
affirmation to yourself 5 times
upon waking and before bed:

I will not compare myself to
others
I am unique and perfectly me

Positive Thoughts

What difficulties have you overcome and how?:

Positive Actions

Write your "past self" a letter.
Be forgiving of any mistakes,
show praise for achievements
and show compassinnate care
for any difficulties

Positive choices

Select a choice & follow it:

I will get my body moving for 10 mins by trying:

Some yoga ☐

Dancing ☐

Stretching ☐

Bike riding ☐

Light jogging ☐

Fitness video ☐

Positive Words

Repeat the following affirmation to yourself 5 times upon waking and before bed:

I am growing through every experience and each day provides a new lesson

Positive Actions

Do something nice for
someone e.g. bake them a cake,
bring them flowers, write them
a thank you note etc...

Positive Intake

Find a new recipe and make
yourself a healthy balanced
meal with plenty of colour
from different
vegetables/fruits

Positive Thoughts

Write down 4 things you are really good at:

Positive Care

Get creative! Try
writing, drawing or
painting

POSITIVITY WORDSEARCH

I	E	E	P	R	P	A	W	E	D	G	I	I	E
S	U	N	A	E	A	U	T	H	E	N	T	I	C
T	T	I	T	F	L	L	I	K	I	N	D	M	T
R	P	N	I	H	C	B	V	E	T	S	D	P	E
E	H	A	E	F	E	S	A	N	V	I	T	G	C
N	I	E	N	U	S	M	T	I	I	S	F	G	N
G	C	T	T	N	G	T	A	E	L	H	R	S	E
T	H	O	U	G	H	T	F	U	L	E	T	M	D
H	T	C	I	E	I	A	C	N	I	H	R	I	I
A	A	S	S	E	R	T	I	V	E	R	L	L	F
P	V	H	O	N	E	S	T	H	Y	U	T	E	N
P	T	N	V	S	G	N	I	R	A	C	N	T	O
Y	L	K	T	U	Y	H	T	R	O	W	K	L	C
H	E	E	C	B	E	V	I	T	A	E	R	C	C

FUN
THOUGHTFUL
RELIABLE
ASSERTIVE
WORTHY
CONFIDENCE
CARING
SMILE
CREATIVE

AUTHENTIC
STRENGTH
KIND
PATIENT
HAPPY
HONEST

Positive Words

Repeat the following affirmation to yourself 5 times upon waking and before bed:

I can achieve anything I put my mind to

Positive choices

Select a choice & follow it:

I will start a new:

Morning routine ☐

Evening routine ☐

For that routine I will:

_____

_____

_____

_____

_____

COLOURING IN

Take some time.....

Positive Care

Get some more rest by
going to bed earlier or
having a lie in

Positive Words

Repeat the following affirmation to yourself 5 times upon waking and before bed:

I am doing my best and my best is good enough

Positive Thoughts

What things/people make you the most happiest and why?:

Positive Actions

Go out for a coffee on your
own or invite someone along.

Positive Care

Make list of things you
want to do and how you
can work towards them

Positive Words

Repeat the following affirmation to yourself 5 times upon waking and before bed:

I will not compare myself to others

I am unique and perfectly me

Positive Thoughts

What difficulties have you overcome and how?:

Positive Actions

Text or call someone you love or care about. Ask how they have been

Positive Thoughts

Name 3 positive attributes about yourself:

Positive Care

Unplug from
technology for the day.

Positive Words

Repeat the following affirmation to yourself 5 times upon waking and before bed:

I choose to be happy and to love myself today

Positive Care

Go for a walk, ideally
where there is nature.
Take your time to listen
to your surroundings as
you walk and try to get
some sunshine

Positive Actions

Genuinely compliment at least
one person today.

Positive Words

Repeat the following affirmation to yourself 5 times upon waking and before bed:

I am strong
I am capable
Today is good day and tomorrow is going to be better

Positive Thoughts

What accomplishments are you proud of?:

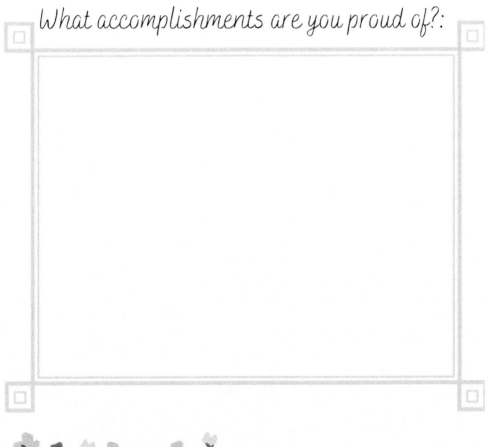

Positive Actions

Donate some unwanted items to charity. This can be clothes/books/food etc....

Positive Words

Repeat the following
affirmation to yourself 5 times
upon waking and before bed:

I accept myself
I believe in myself
Everything I need is within me

Positive Care

Take a long bath or
take the time to slather
on a body cream after a
hot shower

Positive Thoughts

Write down 3 things you are grateful for:

Positive Actions

Try some calming deep belly breathing...
Find a quiet place and get comfortable,
you can sit or lie down. Breathe in deeply
through your nose and let the breath fill
your lungs and lower belly, feeling it rise.
The breathe out slowly through your
mouth. Try to count to 4 in your mind as
you breathe in and the same as you
breathe out. Try to work up to 10 minutes

Reflect and be proud

Think about how much you have accomplished over the past 99 days and what has changed.

Congratulate yourself for making it to day 100 of positivity

Printed in Great Britain
by Amazon

37123432R20056